Fine H
The Top Tools, Best Hairstyles, and
Premier Strategies for Awesome Hair
(and an Even Better Life)
By Holly Houff

Dedication

To you: a lady with fine hair, a caring heart, and a beauty all your own.

Table of Contents
Dedication
Here's to Happy Hair Days

What is Fine Hair?
    Causes | Benefits | Drawbacks

Fine Hair Care
Must-Have Tools
Top 5 Cuts for Fine Hair
    Cap | Crop | Chop | Bob | Layered Lengths | Distraction | More of Me | ... and the #1

Fine Hair Styles and Experts
To Layer or Not to Layer
Finding the Best Fine Hair Stylist
    Tips for Maintaining a Good Relationship With Your Stylist
    Tips for Saving Money on Hair Management

Fine Hair Management and Control
Ayurvedic Approach
Detangling

Hair Coloring
Perms
Swim Care
Hair-Growth Products
Nutritional Supplements
Hair Alternatives
Hair Extensions
How Hair Extensions Could Save Your Life (Seriously)
Wigs and Other Additions

What's in My Shampoo?
Fine Hair Product Reviews
DIY Hair Products
The Future of Shampoo (Will Shampoo Become a Thing of the Past?)
Beauty ... By Your Biome
General Product Tips
Until Next Time

Here's to Happy Hair Days!

This is a book is the result of a one-woman quest to find the best for my baby-fine, straight, limp hair. I've bought armloads of products and run all sorts of sample-of-one experiments to test some wild claims. Yes, for a while I crossed the "fine line" into fine hair obsession! My hope is that all of that hair hassle will help you discover what works best for your hair and your life.

You see, I've always hated my hair.

It began early on, in first grade, when I couldn't get a haircut with feathered, winged layers like my beloved babysitter's. I cursed my genetics. I wasn't alone, though. My mother and two sisters have fine, straight, unmanageable hair. I swore that if I had children, I'd have them with a man with great hair. At least *they* might have a fighting chance at hair that is easy to style and looks good in a lot of different haircuts!

That seems rather silly now, but even the best of us can get fixated on the wrong things for the wrong reasons. That's what happened with my hair. One day I decided that it didn't do much good to hate my hair. A "bad hair day" was becoming my "bad hair life!" How we perceive our hair and overall appearance factors so much into our self-image. So, I needed to figure how I could learn to love my hair. That started a quest to find the absolute best products, strategies, and knowledge to love the hair I have.

In the first version of this book I shared my Top 12 products and strategies. Since products change so fast I've decided to list them all and keep them updated at my website,

FineHairSecrets.com. If you want to know how quickly -- and how wildly! -- things are changing these days, turn to the section new to this version of the book: "The Future of Shampoo."

This book will save you time and effort in locating the best products for fine hair and testing them yourself. You can't change genetics, but you can find the best products and strategies for fine, straight hair right now.

While preparing this updated book I spoke to my stylist and friend, Lori Jo Holloran. Lori has a flourishing business in two locations (Norfolk, Virginia, and Asheville, North Carolina) and has a roster of clients throughout the Mid-Atlantic.

I asked her, "What are you top two tips for women with fine, thin, hair?" She said:

1. Caruso rollers to the curl the hair. Use saltwater steam to make them stay. [See the section: Must-Have Tools]

2. No long hair and no dark colors [...] get a nice, short cut with a fringe and highlights to keep the contrast of your hair and scalp minimal.

Awesome, I said. Then I asked, "What would be your No. 1 life tip?" (Yes, I'm nosy that way). She said, "Do what you love! Do not put worth in the judgment of others, and smile because it is the one thing that makes everyone look good and feel good."

I couldn't agree more. Maybe that's why we're friends!

Thank you for reading because it helps me do what I love: writing. It's my hope that you, too, do what you love. This book will help you make peace with your hair. I hope it also helps you make peace with anything real or imagined that's stopping you from being YOU, because that is truly the first step to happy days ahead.

I look forward to hearing from you, and all about your happy hair days.

Sincerely,

Holly Houff
Copyright 2006-2014

Disclaimer

This book is not intended as medical advice. If you are experiencing hair loss, see a doctor.

This book is personal opinion based on numerous and costly personal product, technique, and experimental trials. Consult your doctor, dermatologist, or professional hairstylist for more information. All trade names of companies and other products are trademarks, registered trademarks, or trade names of their respective holders and have been used in an editorial fashion only, with no intention of infringement of any kind.

Also, girl, take note: Don't let your hair get you down. Ever.

What Is Fine Hair?

"Fine" refers to the diameter of a single strand of your hair. Fine hair comes in two broad categories: fine hair that is abundant (meaning, you have a lot of fine hair per square inch), or fine hair that is small in diameter and top of that, you don't have a lot of it. Sometimes it's called "thinning" hair, but I can assure you that I called it "a curse." I have the latter -- not a lot of hair, and hair so fine and straight that it feels like soft rabbit hair. Which is great, except rabbits aren't really known for their fashionable hairstyles.

Causes of Fine, Thin Hair

You can get fine, baby fine, or thin hair from your parents (genetically) or from medical issues (such as fighting cancer or managing ongoing thyroid disease). You might even have a combination, like me (genetically fine hair not helped by ongoing hypothyroidism). Age, diet, stress, medication, and environmental factors can make fine but abundant hair begin to thin, and appear sparse in density. Of course, if you notice dramatic changes in your hair you need to see a doctor.

Benefits of Fine Hair
Fine, straight hair does offer some benefits. When healthy and properly cared for, it can shine and shimmer like fine-spun gold or bronze. Fine, straight hair is softer than your favorite sweater and a delight to touch. Many people associate fine, silky hair with youth and femininity. Who would argue with that?

Drawbacks
Of course there are plenty of drawbacks, too. But you knew that already! The most common complaint with fine hair is limpness. Or the tangles. Or the inability to hold a curl.

Or that it takes forever to grow. Or something else.

Must-Have Tools

Before you make changes to your hair, you need to make sure you're using the right tools.

I will get into detail in all these later in the book.

Drying Hair
Even though your hair probably dries quickly by itself, you'll need a hair dryer to really maximize its volume.

Pick a hair dryer that ideally has:
- Length enough to be held comfortably away from your scalp -- you don't want to risk getting your hair tangled in the exhaust end (travel hair dryers, which are a lot smaller, always seem to do this

to my hair)

- A diffuser extension (concentrator nozzle) to focus air on smaller sections of your roots at a time

- A "cool shot" feature to set hair

If you are deciding between heat levels, choose a device that has a high heat setting. It is better to expose your hair to high heat for short period of time rather than expose to low heat for a longer amount of time. Minimize the amount of heat you give your hair by being as efficient as possible.

I once yearned for the CHI Ceramic Ionic Hair Dryer, the limousine of hair dryers, which is said to be lightweight and quiet. Eventually I decided it was too expensive and did not buy it. If you can afford it, spring for a professional-grade hair dryer. The craftsmanship is better and it should last longer because it is built for ongoing use. As you know hairdryers can be noisy, and that can be bad for your ears.

Don't fret, though, because you don't have to spend a lot of money to buy a good hairdryer. I used a very inexpensive hairdryer made by Revlon -- and it lasted 12 years! Twelve years! They don't make that model anymore. Like anything else, hairdryers are rotated in and out of fashion. That's good news for you frugal shoppers because you can even find a decent hairdryer second-hand.

Look for one with the attributes above. (I purchased one at a yard sale! Sometimes people will part with a quality product that is in a color that was hot a few years ago but looks dated now.) If you get one secondhand, turn it on first (if you can) to test the noise levels.

Styling
Rounded brush
It's easy for fine hair to become tangled in rounded brushes, but when used correctly they seem to do the best job. Choose one with widely-spaced teeth with soft or flexible bristles. Also good is a well-worn bristle brush: the softer bristles are easier on the hair if you don't do a lot of brushing.

Hot Rollers
Steam-driven Caruso rollers are ideal for adding maximum body, even if you plan to brush your hair out straight afterwards.

Curling Iron
Some argue that a curling iron is the most damaging of all tools for fine hair.

Personally, it's my No. 1 styling choice. Choose a curling iron with a high heat setting. Use the highest heat for the least amount of time to avoid hair cuticle damage. A decent curling iron is a great tool for turning under or flipping up ends.

Other styling tool options

Traditional sponge rollers
If you desire a really curly look and can manage to sleep in them, traditional sponge rollers work wonders. Find them at your nearest drugstore. Avoid Velcro rollers -- they tangle faster than you can snap your fingers! Instead, go for the ones made of cushiony pink foam, or for traditional, smooth plastic rollers that you attach with bobby pins. Undo them when your hair is dry, then flip your head over and gently finger-comb for the most natural look. Set with hairspray.

Crimpers

Crimpers are great for a funky look, but again, choose one with high heat and use it for just as long as absolutely necessary to avoid damaging your hair.

Detangling and Teasing

- Fine-tooth comb for teasing

- Wide-tooth comb for detangling

- General-purpose comb (optional, look for one with both kinds of teeth)

Other Supplies

Fine Mist Water Spray Bottle

One trick is to have a fine-mist water spray bottle available mid-day to lightly spritz your hair to reactive your styling products. Your aim is to lightly wet the surface layers with the fine drops but to keep the balance of your style dry. Too much and you'll droop! You can find these at any drugstore. Just be certain it can produce a light mist!

Top 7 Hairstyles for Fine Hair

Hairstyle trends come and go. Still, there are some that will flatter your hair. First, fine hair looks best when it is one short length. The shorter the hair and the more it remains one length the thicker its appearance. But sometimes that gets boring. Here are five hairstyles you'll enjoy in the hands of a skilled stylist:

1. The Cap: This is also known as a "bowl cut" since it is an all-bangs approach. This cut looks best on young people and children, but don't be afraid to experiment. If

you are a petite person with petite features you're an ideal candidate for this cut, you cutie-pie!

2. The Crop: A crop cut refers to almost any short, tapered cut. These hairstyles draw attention to your eyes and skin. Crops look cool on younger women (and those who don't worry about double chins), but don't let age limit you. The most important part of a crop cut is the attitude: YES, I'm rockin' this look.

3. The Chop: The chop is very popular and has enduring fans. It is a variation on a basic bob (of various length). Some versions include irregular lengths. You can emphasize ends for a fun, contemporary look. Sometimes the shaggy ends on an irregularly cut style can hide the fact that you're

due for a haircut for a week or so! This hairstyle looks really hot if you play it up with color (more on that later!)

4. The Bob: This classic cut comes in a thousand variations. It can range in length from short (earlobe length) to longer (several inches down the neck). You can keep a bob cut one length or get it stacked. One length is classic, neat, and sleek. Stacking a bob can make hair look a little fuller.

5. The Lightly Layered Mid-Length: You can go just to, or even below, the shoulder with a smart shape and regular ends. It may or may not include bangs. (This varies tremendously depending on your specific situation, e.g., cowlicks, texture, and amount of hair.) One of my favorite cuts is a

combination of a crop and the layered mid-length ... cropped in the back and then gradually getting longer on a diagonal angle to frame my round face in a mid-length, layered bob.

6. The Distraction: I use this hairstyle about once a week, and you can, too. Comb your hair back, pin it in place, and then work to distract the eye away from your hair. This can be achieved with a dramatic hair accessory or hat. Do not dismiss this as a cop-out. Rather, this is a practical strategy to celebrate your individual style and feel good about yourself. (It can also significantly reduce getting-ready time!) I will talk more about accessories and hats in a moment.

7. More of Me: Never discount the power of clip-ons, extensions,

partial wigs, and even full wigs. Often, it is assumed that if you are using hair extensions or wigs, you must either be vain ... or seriously ill. By being more open about these embellishments we'll all feel better about using them. What woman hasn't used a push-up bra? Lipstick? And to those who pooh-pooh it by saying, "Oh, I'd never use fake hair!" -- well, honey, you're missing out on some fun. More on that later, too.

8. The #1: Forget all of the previously mentioned hairstyles. What you should ALWAYS get is "the Number 1." Which hairstyle is that, you ask? It is the attitude that you are beautiful -- *no matter what! I'll say it again. You, your hair -- everything about you is beautiful.*

You might not see this because it is easy to fixate our flaws. I know I've been guilty of this. I've wasted too much time and emotional effort focusing on flaws. Don't let this happen to you. Don't allow another day to pass before you decide to fixate instead on your gifts. Practice thinking this way if you must. No one will remember you because of your hair. They will remember you because of YOU. Start being the best you possible: Start loving yourself. Give yourself credit. Forgive yourself. Count your blessings. We ladies don't do enough of that.

Okay, girl. I'm totally serious about all that. I can't stress it enough. But, let's back to it, shall we?

Other Hairstyle Strategies

Wearing your hair sleek and close to your head is another strategy that works to give the illusion of more hair. If your hair is long enough to tuck behind your ears, this can give the illusion of more hair. A small amount can drop down into your face for a sexy moment.

Long bangs can be difficult with fine hair if you don't have a lot of it. If you have enough hair volume, bangs can be cut into slight layers to frame your face.

A slightly asymmetrical cut can make hair look thicker if you put visual emphasis on the thicker side. Zigzag parts are fun sometimes, too.

When all else fails and you're just completely sick of your hair, there are still plenty of options. See the preceding Distraction/More of Me strategies. First, you can wrap your hair up in a classic un-do that looks sleek and gets it all off your face (add "fake" hair if necessary).

Pulling your hair up is a great choice when the weather is hot and humid -- the worst weather for fine, limp hair.

Secondly, you can always use stylish hair clips. They can be fun and take emphasis away from the hair itself. I'm always on the lookout for accoutrements that aren't too heavy or too big to stay in fine hair. Often these are made for little girls. The best I've found are barrettes for little girls made by a company called "No Slippy Hair Clippy." When this book was first released, the company only made barrettes for kids (I was a fan of the big flower clip). I'm happy to report that they now make hair clips for teens and women, too. See: hairclippy.com.

And of course, no matter the season, don't dismiss the power of a stylish hat! In my opinion, hats are the epitome of good style and just aren't worn enough today. A stylish hat can literally make an outfit -- and it is a great solution to hair blahs! Just wear your hair tied back neatly underneath. Or not (depends on the hat!)

If you're STILL fed up with your hair, remember some simple but profound advice my mother gave me (in addition to my genes for fine, thin hair): "Smile, and no one will notice."

To Layer or Not to Layer...? That Is the Question -- for Your Hairstylist

Layers can make abundant fine hair look awesome. Layers have even worked well on my hair, and I have thinning hair. But you need to have a sensitive hair stylist who won't go crazy and create too many layers. This can destroy the line of the haircut. End result: your hair looks flatter and thinner than before!

The same holds true for cuts using a razor. There is a fine line (pardon the pun) between a good thing and *too much* of a good thing. This is why it's important to find a stylist you like and trust and stay with him or her. Your stylist will learn what works best for your hair. Do your stylist a favor and be open to trying new things with your hair. By keeping a relationship with the person who cuts your hair, you'll automatically increase your chances of getting the best haircuts for your specific look and lifestyle.

Finding the Best Fine Hair Stylist

Seasoned Professional

Should you pay a lot for the services of a hairstylist? That depends on your budget. If you can afford an experienced professional you like, it's worth it because they've spent years learning the craft. Besides: professionals are always worth the money. Just ask anyone who tried to install their own toilet. (I'd tell you that messy tale, but, this isn't the time or place!) You also benefit from the ongoing relationship and possible friendship that may develop. Choosing to support an independent stylist (versus a national hair cutting chain) is a great way to keep dollars circulating in your local economy, too. Tip well!

A great way to start is the most obvious: ask around. Ask friends and family members with fine hair where they have their hair done (if you like it). You can also approach strangers who appear to have hair of a similar texture and amount as yours (and whose hair you admire). You might have heard that people won't reveal their stylist for fear that the stylist will be overrun with bookings or raise their prices. However, it has been my experience that if you are polite most people are flattered that you've admired their hair and will gladly tell you (even when I lived in New York City!) If your stylist does become more popular it only benefits you: The more experience he or she gets with fine hair, the faster and better they'll be able to treat you!

If you are disappointed to learn that the stylist you've found is more expensive than you thought, consider it a good sign: stylists charge what people will pay, and, the more people willing to pay usually indicates their skill level. Don't feel pressured to go back if you don't think you received value in proportion to the service offered.

A strategy to reducing your cost is to add a few weeks extra between appointments. If you're respectful of your stylist's overhead costs you may be able to work out a partial trade or other exchange. Be sure to discuss this before you use their services. (I've seen it done afterward and it is poorly received!) Don't be offended if a trade cannot be offered. You never know his or her circumstances. Again, tip well, especially if you work out a trade!

Recent Graduate or Apprentice

Another option is to look for local beautician schools or salon training centers nearby. My grandfather, who was a barber, used to say that volunteering your head of hair to a student was one of the best things you could do to support others if you're on a tight budget. I've done this during lean times as a writer and had the good fortune to get some excellent cuts at a fraction of the cost. Ask for a student who is known for or is concentrating on fine hair (if you get the option -- some schools or training salons have a policy to assign the next student in line). If you have a choice here's a simple and effective trick: Find and request the student who has fine hair. He or she will be more sensitive to your particular needs.

There are two major drawbacks to getting your hair cut in a beautician school or salon training center. The first is the investment in time, because instructors need to review each step of the process and advise the student as they go along. Depending on the student, this can significantly extend the time necessary for your appointment. The other drawback is that they graduate! So, just as they are getting good they depart. If you find a student you really like do not be shy about giving him or her your contact information. When he or she lands their first job they will be happy to have a new client. Don't be shy!

Fine Hair Care - Ayurvedic Approach

Ayurvedic tradition has its roots in India. According to the tradition, our body types (called "doshas") fall into three categories: vata, pitta, and kapha. These types refer to our overall body shape, mind-body state, and natural equilibrium. As a medical system it has been used for more than 5,000 years, now in conjunction with modern medicine. Good ideas never go out of style, right?

According to the tradition, people with fine and thinning hair are pitta-prominent. The recommended treatment is a regular massage of the scalp with coconut oil. The theory is that the massage cools the Pitta-energy and balances the energy system in your body. To do it properly it is recommended that Ayurvedic oils and herbs be used for any kind of body treatments (in this case, coconut). In my opinion, you don't need the Ayurvedic name in front of the oil for it to work.

I've experimented using pure coconut oil with an octopus-shaped scalp massager I purchased online. (If you're curious, it is shaped like an octopus and the head forms the handle and its wire "arms" massage your head.) It is a real treat but not something I used regularly after experimenting with other things, so I gave it away. You don't need a fancy massager -- your fingers will do just fine.

Heat the oil on the stove or in the microwave. Make sure it is not too hot! Wet your hair and then massage your hair follicles with the warmed oil for several minutes and the rest of your hair if you want, too. Then wrap a towel around your head and let it soak into your scalp for 30-40 minutes. You can even leave it overnight if you protect your sheets with a towel. (Pro tip: This treatment is even better if you can have someone give you the scalp massage!)

According to tradition this process "feeds" the hair follicles.

I didn't notice a big difference in my hair with regular application of coconut oil. It did seem to have more shine. Maybe your results will be better. However, I sure looked forward to the massage! As a way to manage stress, I believe massage and relaxation with essential oils or music to produce a "spa experience" can indirectly lead to healthier hair. At the very least it provided me with an overall relaxing health boost and some "me time." Indulge yourself!

Fine Hair Care - Detangling

Fine hair can be smooth and silky like no other hair type -- but this also means it will tangle, knot, and break faster than any other hair type, too. It is fragile!

The best way to approach detangling your hair is to do it with the least amount of pulling. First, towel-dry your hair gently. If you are really susceptible to tangles, use a rinse conditioner. Work it into your hair and leave it in as you comb out your hair in the shower. You'll need a good wide-tooth comb.

Depending on your preference, use a detangling spray. There are several on the market. My favorite, hands down, is Little Sprout Miracle Detangler.

Start at the bottom, *not the top*, of your head. Work your way up. This avoids creating knots. This seems obvious but I've seen many people with fine hair go top-to-bottom (and have memories of this as a kid) and end up ripping out hair. If you do it right, no hair should rip at all!

Never brush wet hair -- you're just asking for trouble! Brushing will stretch wet hair. Brushing wet hair will damage it -- if it doesn't outright tangle it or pull it out!

A great deal of volume can be added by using a hairdryer and styling aids. Therefore, I recommend that you do your detangling routine in the morning (or before going out in the evening) so you can continue your styling. If you insist on showering before bed (not recommended), make sure to comb your hair thoroughly before climbing into bed.

Fine Hair Care - Coloring

I love coloring my hair -- it is the perfect, non-fattening treat to lift the spirits. You can have a lot of fun with drugstore washable coloring kits (the kind of color that washes out after several shampoos). But, if you're not playing around and seeking something more permanent, in my opinion, coloring is best left to the experts

Color can, literally, fatten up the hair (the opposite is true of bleaching). Hair color actually contains chemical properties that slightly puff up each strand of hair. This helps it feel fuller.

Strategically applied color can also add interest and depth to any haircut. Two colors can give the illusion of more hair.

You can create this by adding highlights, lowlights, or even two shades of the same hair color.

It is important to avoid solutions that contain peroxide. You want to avoid agents that strip the cuticle down. These are often found in peroxide-based formulas on the blond end of the color spectrum. Red hair color is more difficult to maintain because it washes out easily. My stylist explained that red color molecules are bigger than other shades and can't "grip" like the others. Again, a professional knows more about the chemical components of a particular color and can give advice individual to you. For example, grey hairs have a different texture and structure that affects their ability to hold color.

Best advice: Step far, far away from the bleach! It will eat away at your fragile hair and make its texture rough and brittle. Not to mention it turns your hair nasty shades of undesirable colors! I'd also avoid the "more natural" option of using lemon juice in your hair to lighten it. Lemon juice is also corrosive to the hair follicle -- easy for someone with plenty of hair to spare, but not for people with fine hair! Find a professional to guide you to a color (or colors) that won't strip away your hair strand.

If you decide to do it yourself and want something more permanent, I'd recommend hair colors formulated with natural ingredients. I like Herbatint because it uses rosemary, cinchona, and walnut husk to gently deposit color. It also doesn't give that one-color-all-over look that a lot of colors from drugstores deliver. It is also 100% plant-based, so nothing gross ends up in your hair!

Fine Hair Care - Perms

I had a perm in my hair for several years and yes, I lived to tell the tale.

Happily, there have been significant changes in the chemical makeup of perms. Now they are less drying and not as harsh on delicate fine hair as they once were. Again, I think it is worth it to invest in a professional stylist's application. Ask for a "body wave" if you don't want tight ringlets.

Body perms are the best to give an overall boost to the hair's appearance. In my experience a good haircut with select layers can give straight, fine hair almost as much volume as a perm without too many harsh chemicals.

Don't be fooling into perming and coloring your hair at the same time. No matter the advancement in both types of products, used together they are likely to ruin your hair! It is just too many competing chemicals changing the physical structure of each individual hair strand.

A common mistake when styling permed hair with hot rollers is to place the rollers along the same direction as the perm rods. This can lead to clear divides of blank patches on the scalp showing through! Instead, experiment laying the hot rollers like bricks over the original perm rod route. In other words, overlap the rollers to look like bricks in a wall. Remove the curlers only when they are completely cool. Use a light amount of mousse or spray gel before you dry and/or curl your hair. Set the curl with a spritz of hairspray. If you do a lot of this, do yourself a favor and buy a handheld mirror so you can more easily see how they lie in the back.

Fine Hair Care -- Swimming

Chlorine water can ruin fine hair feaster than you can dive into it! I know because I was on the swim team in high school. During my sophomore year my hair was a pale shade of green and the texture of dry, brittle cotton candy thanks to a perm and the pool. My poor hair broke off in chunks. Not a good look!

(Side note: Sometimes green can be fun. As of this writing I have two intentional streaks of peacock green in my hair thanks to Lori. This section focuses on avoiding unintentional green hair!)

Avoiding Damage

First, realize that most chlorine-reducing shampoos are very harsh in their own right. These shampoos are typically created for "normal" hair and so contain oils and residues too heavy for fine hair.

I'd recommend avoiding all of them. They work by chemically stripping your hair. Anything that further reduces the size of the hair cuticle is bad news.

The solution is easy and inexpensive. First, invest in a high-quality swimming cap. I own two. One is a silicone cap. The other is made of nylon and elastane (elastic, similar to Lycra). Yes, these cost a little more than basic rubber caps but are worth every penny because they go both on and off your head without pulling out your hair. (If you've used cheap rubber swimming caps you know what I'm talking about!)

Next, make sure that you thoroughly wet your hair in regular water and cover it in conditioner *before* you get into the pool. This forces your hair cuticle to soak up clean water first instead of pool water. You can use cheap conditioner here because the goal is to create a barrier. Put it on thick and work it into your hair.

By wetting your hair, covering it with conditioner, and topping it off with a swimming cap, you can prevent nearly all chlorine damage. Using this strategy I've discovered you can greatly eliminate or even skip the expensive chlorine-reducing shampoos. Instead, use can rinse off all the conditioner then use your preferred shampoo formulated for fine hair.

If you don't want to wear a cap, at least consider wetting your hair before going into the pool.

Already Damaged

Believe me, I've tried every protein mix, spritz, and spray. Don't waste your money! You cannot undo chlorine damage. If your hair already is damaged by the pool (a good indication is that it feels like cotton candy and breaks easily) you basically have one option: Cut your hair. Cut as much as you feel comfortable doing and take good care of your hair as it grows out. Regular trims will keep removing the damaged hair and keeping new growth looking good.

Hair-Growth Products

If you are losing your hair in a particular pattern or area of your scalp or are losing hair at an alarming rate ***you need to see a doctor. This point cannot be stressed enough because this could indicate more serious problems.***

If you are curious enough to try one of the hair-growth products on the market, do not be taken in by snake-oil salesmen! Stick with medically regulated products like Propecia or Rogain (note: speak to your doctor first). Even though these are sold over the counter there is the risk that they'll interfere with other drugs you may be taking. These drugs don't work for everyone and stop working when you stop using them. Sorry, but these products will do nothing to simply increase naturally fine hair.

Supplements

Generally, I would avoid most supplements or supplement combos that claim to be just for your hair. Most of what is inside can be obtained less expensively through a carefully planned, balanced diet. A catch-all vitamin is probably fine for your overall health and can't hurt your hair.

I am a big supporter of natural health approaches and herbs. Yet, you must be cautious and speak to a doctor before adding any herbs into your diet in large quantities because they can interfere with the effectiveness of prescription drugs or be problematic in large doses. Compare brands and do your research so you know what -- if any -- dietary recommendations are in place for a particular herb. As the old truism goes, you get what you pay for.

Avoid medicine or unregulated supplements available online from another country. Regulations there might not be as strict about what is inside or about revealing effects. If you want to get something unavailable in the U.S., look for a Canadian importer. I used them to purchase UVB sunscreen before it was widely added to sunscreens in the States.

Herbs purported to increase and stimulate hair growth include:

fenugreek, thyme, sage, ivy burdock, and horsetail (from personal experience I can tell you that fenugreek gives you "hippy body odor" to use the words of a friend). I didn't see significant differences during a three-month experiment using all of these.

Of this experimental period (three months on each supplement) there was one exception: biotin. I noticed less hair left in my comb. Coincidentally, this is the natural recommendation my stylist made. The recommended dosage is 2.5 milligrams a day according to this article on *The Huffington Post*. Note: it is possible to overdose and there can be consequences such as "slower release of insulin, skin rashes, lower vitamin C and B6 levels and high blood sugar levels." So take precautions and do not overdo it!

Hair Extensions

Hair extensions come in three broad categories. First, the ultra-cheap clip-ons. You can find these extensions at the drugstore or (gasp!) some street fairs or bazaars. I once saw a selection of hair extensions in downtown Los Angele's garment district. I though they looked like they were made of llama hair -- wiry, smelly, and certainly not flattering for anyone! You've probably seen better quality clip-ons at your local drugstore. They are made of artificial fibers and come in a very limited selection of colors and shades. Some have faux scrunchies, rubber bands, or other clips to hide their attachment. You might get lucky and find some that are passable under certain light conditions (a dark restaurant or bar, for instance). Yes, you can wear them as part of a costume, or maybe for an evening out. They probably won't pass for daily wear.

How Hair Extensions Might Save Your Life

Don't dismiss the humble drugstore hair extension. It might literally save your life. Seriously.

The catch is the context. Do you ride a bicycle to work or for play? Okay, there is a happy face/frowny face aspect to why a drugstore hair extension might save your life. We have a dose of sexism to thank. I am hopeful this trend is changing as more of us ladies are choosing to ride our bikes for pleasure, exercise, and transportation.

It turns out that drivers are more likely to slow down and safely pass female cyclists. Experiments in both the U.K. and U.S. confirm it. Is it because drivers are being polite? Or is it because women on bikes are subconsciously deemed less experienced and prone to greater erratic behavior on the road? Read about the studies at the site TotalWomensCycling.com.

If you are like me and enjoy riding your bike consider investing in both an inexpensive fake ponytail and/or a helmet to show off your hair. Helmets made just for ponytails are featured in a series called "Hairport," by Specialized. They probably don't know about these studies but do know that having your hair off your neck makes for a more enjoyable ride! (By the way, helmets are a whole other fascinating discussion as they relate to bicycling adoption. This isn't the place for that but you can find a controversial take on the matter -- no helmets at all! -- at the [*New York Times*](New York Times).)

More Expensive Hair Extensions

The second kind of hair extension is much more expensive. They come either as clip-ons or are stitched and glued into your natural hair. I will discuss both.

The more expensive clip-on extensions are really good -- and used more widely than you imagine. They can add fullness, length, or both depending on what you choose and how you attach them. I recommend having your stylist attach them the first time you use them so you can see the best way to use them.

Better quality clip-on extensions are easy to put on and take off they make a great addition to your assortment of hair products. They can be worn regularly, even daily if you are motivated to do so and are willing to eventually replace them (just like your favorite sweater they eventually). Since high-end clip-ons are typically made of human hair you will treat them similarly to your own hair. If you plan to dye them to match your hair make sure to order a shade lighter than your natural color. This works better for color.

When using clip-on extensions you can slightly back-comb and tease the individual strands. (Be sure that all back-combing is out before you shampoo to avoid tangles.) You should arrange the clips around the back of the skull and make sure that there aren't any bulges that you can see or feel for the most natural look.

Note: If your hair is so fine and thinning that it would be difficult to hide the weft that attaches the hair extension to your scalp, this might not be the best option. In this case, consider a fuller option — a wiglet, chignon, pastiche, cascade (various types of wigs and wig styles). Don't be embarrassed -- hairpieces have been fashionable accessories since the dawn of time!

One extension (reported to have been used in Victoria Secret fashion shows) is Garland Drake. They offer all kinds of hair extensions, from bangs to pieces that add length and volume. For a small fee you can request samples to get the right match for your hair.

Screen siren and ageless beauty Raquel Welch is such a fan of clip-on extensions and wigs that she developed her own signature line! These are moderately priced and you can find them online and through QVC. Expect to invest a little money to get something that works for you.

Braid-in Extensions

I once spent a small fortune and several hours to get a head full of braided and glued extensions. I have to admit: the end result gave me the kind of hair I always wanted! I *loved* the results! But, it is a long, expensive process and not without some pitfalls.

The way it works is that they section your hair into very small chunks around the top of your head. Then the stylist braids and glues real (or in my case, fake) hair to your natural hair. I chose fake hair because it lasted a little longer and I wanted to maximize the wear. (And hey, it was really shiny!) The stylist then selected a combination of strands from various color collections and mixed the multiple colors to create a close match to my own hair. The sections of braid and glue were small, only about 1/8 inch. Eventually there was so much "fake" hair that it covered up the tiny braids attached to my natural hair. The process took close to six hours! The labor involved is why it was so expensive, but also because of the price of the extensions themselves.

TIP: If you decide to get these kinds of extensions, make sure you tip your stylist really, really well! I'd recommend at least 30% for something as laborious and time consuming as this. If in doubt, tip more.

Maintenance includes using a special kind of shampoo so that the glue on the braids doesn't flake or lose its adhesive properties. A minor inconvenience arises when your head itches. As your natural hair grows out there is a visible line between the thin amount of hair on the top and crown of your head and the mysteriously much thicker volume of hair below.

Overall, I loved my extensions and would happily have them all the time if my budget allowed. However, one of the most embarrassing moments was when I was making out with a date. He ran his hands over the surface of my hair and the kissing continued. Suddenly he grabbed my head with both hands under my ears to pull me passionately closer. This backfired. He immediately retracted like he'd touched a hot coal. "What is *that in your hair*?" I guess it surprised him. I felt a bit shallow to admit they were hair extensions and that was a buzzkill. In hindsight I should've acted like, "So what?" and continued.

SIDE NOTE: If you have just a few clips of hair extensions it is really easy to play it off as "oh, that's just a clip I put in my hair to style it."

ANOTHER SIDE NOTE: That guy was a fussy jerk.

Braid-in extensions aren't forever, either. They have a recommended lifespan of three months. Eventually your natural hair grows out enough that the braids slide down and fall out. Before they fall out they will leave an inch or so of "skinny" hair at your scalp and then -- poof! -- much thicker hair below. This isn't a natural look. Plus, at this stage people can more easily see the braids and glue. It looks a bit gross and pokes out between your real hair. Trust me. Since I'd spent so much money on them I chose to keep them in for just over a year! Eventually, my natural hair broke off. My advice: if you go this route have the budget to keep it up at the recommended rate. Don't be cheap and try to extend the lifespan!

Should I Feel Embarrassed to Wear Fake Hair?

Of course not! Say it loud and proud if you want. I know this isn't everyone's style but there is no sense in carrying any shame. If wearing some additional "hair help" makes you feel better than that is all that matters.

What's in My Shampoo?

Almost everyone agrees animal testing in cosmetics is cruel and unnecessary. But do you know if you hair product is MADE from animals? If this is important to you check your labels.

A
Acetate (Retinol) an aliphatic alcohol that can be sourced from fish oil (e.g., shark liver oil), egg yolks, or butter. Sometimes this is synthetic.

B
Biotin is found in every living cell; often sourced in bulk from milk or yeast.

C
Cetyl Alcohol is a wax found in spermaceti from sperm whales or dolphins

Cetyl Palmitate is a waxy oil derived from the heads of sperm whales or dolphins

Collagen is a protein usually derived from animal tissue

D
Depanthenol is a vitamin complex mostly sourced from animals, but occasionally synthetic. Less expensive shampoos are more likely to use animal-sourced vitamins.

G
Glycerin is usually an animal fat byproduct. Sometimes glycerin can be made from vegetable sources.

L
Lanolin is produced by the oil glands of sheep and extracted from their wool.

P
Panthenol (see depanthenol)

Q
Quaternium 27 is made from the fat of cows, sheep, pigs, and occasionally dogs and cats from shelters

R
Retinol (see acetate)

S
Stearyl Alcohol is a mixture of solid alcohols, possibly sourced from sperm whale oil

There is a reason you don't know these words. Manufacturers don't want to advertise these ingredients! To avoid personal-care items with these ingredients, buy items that are clearly labeled with "no animal ingredients" or "vegan." Download one of many free apps, such as *Is It Vegan?* by Conner Burggraf, to scan an item and verify. Most of this app concerns food but is expanding into other products, too.

Another free resource is the search at PETA (People for the Ethical Treatment of Animals) called "Beauty Without Bunnies: Search for Cruelty Free Companies".

NOTE: You may need to pay extra for animal-free products. If you can't afford to pay extra consider you have three choices:

1. reducing the overall amount of product you use

2. look for a DIY options, explored next

3. await the shampoo-less future, explored next

General Product Tips for Baby Fine and Fine Hair

When I first published this ebook in 2006 I had tested more than 100 products and found the Top 12 products that work to support and improve fine, limp, and thinning hair. One for each month! I ranked them based on fragrance, price, and -- most importantly -- performance. I approached this from the consumer's standpoint and did my best to report on known ingredients, availability, and approximate prices. I also included the best places to buy these products online since not all brands I discovered while living in New York City were available nationwide.

In the intervening years there have been numerous changes. Some products were discontinued. Others changed price, lessening or negating their overall value. So, for this latest version I will direct you to my website and mailing list to see my up-to-date current favorite products. Use it to find your next "favorite" beauty supply! Just head over to **FineHairSecrets.com**.

That said, there are some perennial tips to help you look for products that perform well and keep you looking your best:

Shampoo

- Less, much less, is more. Use about half the recommended amount. Make sure to lather it up rather than just running it through your hair. This will do the job and save you money.

- You don't have to use a deep-cleansing shampoo for buildup unless you regularly use a really cheap shampoo-conditioner combination.

- Avoid products labeled as "heavy moisturizing" and cautiously approach those labeled "for normal hair." These products tend to be too heavy and weigh baby fine hair down.

Conditioner

- Choose a lightweight rinse conditioner or skip it altogether

- Less is more; concentrate on the very tips of your hair instead of the last inch(es)

- Leave on for a least a minute to maximize its effectiveness

- Look for a product that easily rises out -- generally speaking, the fewer the ingredients, the lighter the conditioner

- Occasionally do an all-over condition and make sure you rinse it well

Products

Avoid heavy gels, styling waxes, or pomades.

Limit or totally avoid most "gloss" or "shine" sprays because they weigh your hair down and can make it look dirty. Instead, read the next section because something you probably have in your kitchen right now will keep your hair shiny and full of body.

If you want to experiment, spray these on one side of your hair (dry hair only). Any more than a few spritzes risks weighing down any body you've managed to create.

DIY Hair Products

In the last section, I told you chances were good you already have something in your kitchen that will improve the shine of you hair without weighing it down. That product is vinegar. Apple cider vinegar is preferred. I came to this conclusion once I started experimenting with the creative side of do-it-yourself hair care.

There are several reasons you might decide to take matters into your own hands and create your own hair products. You might want to control the ingredients to avoid unnecessary chemicals or fragrances. Or, you might just be the crafty kind who enjoys the creativity that comes from making your own recipe. Sometimes, making your own hair products can be economical, too.

Here are some ideas to get you started.

No Poo "Shampoo"
I credit Lindsey of the blog High Heels and Training Wheels for introducing me

to the idea of "No Poo". No, it doesn't have to do with *that*! Lindsey uses just two ingredients to create a hair cleaner that only needs to be applied once a week: baking soda plus apple cider vinegar. (Think of the money you could save!) She has a revised version of the recipe that uses honey, too. Both variations work by working with the natural oils on your scalp.

You should read Lindsey's post, linked above, to get the details. Here is the general gist of it. First: it isn't a science, so you can eyeball the ingredients. Transfer your baking soda to a watertight container that you can keep in the bathroom. This will prevent it from getting moist. Find an inexpensive spray bottle you can fill with vinegar. Vinegar is used because it seals the cuticle of your hair and makes it shinier.

STEP 1: Moisten your hair completely.

STEP 2: Measure out approximately 1 tablespoon of baking soda in your palm.

STEP 3: Work the baking soda into your hair, concentrating on the roots and scalp. No need to work it down the length of your hair.

STEP 4: Let it set for a minute or two. You can suds up or shave while you wait.

STEP 5: Rinse well and get out of the shower.

STEP 6: Spray apple cider down the length of your hair. Yes, it will smell when you spray it but not once your hair is dried.

STEP 7: Comb and style as desired!

A couple of notes: First, it will take some time for you hair and scalp to adjust to this process. So, don't start this once a week plan if you have an upcoming wedding or special event. Second, it will take some experimentation to determine what amounts and frequency work best for you. TIP: Fine hair looks limp and matted more quickly when scalp oils make it "dirty," so, start washing with this method on a daily basis and then taper down to what works best for you.

Baby Fine Banana Treatment
This fine hair fattener comes from Audrey Davis-Sivasothy, author of *Hair Care Rehab: The Ultimate Hair Repair and Reconditioning Manual*. This temporary fix will help plump up fine hair (at least until your next shampoo). It is also a nice treat for your hair after swimming in chlorine.

STEP 1: Obtain the following ingredients: (2) ripe bananas; (2) eggs; (3) tablespoons honey; (3) tablespoons olive oil; (1/2) cup of hair conditioner. Note: Generic products work just as well as more expensive options.

STEP 2: Combine all in the blender (minus the egg shells) and blend well. You can compost the egg shells for healthier garden soil.

STEP 3: Slather all onto wet hair.

STEP 4: Wait 20-30 minutes and then rinse well with cool water.

Natural Hair Spray/Volumizer

This is definitely a less-is-more technique from WellnessMama.com, but it can be a substitute for more expensive hairsprays and volumizers. It uses white sugar, which is terrible for your body but great for your hair!

STEP 1: Buy, or wash and reuse a hairspray bottle.

STEP 2: Obtain the following ingredients: (1.5) cups of water; (2) tablespoons of white sugar; (1) tablespoon higher-proof alcohol (she recommends spiced rum for the scent). Optionally, you can collect and use your favorite essential oil for fragrance.

STEP 3: Boil the water and dissolve the sugar in it.

STEP 4: Allow the water to cool to room temperature. Add the alcohol, and the essential oil if you're using one.

STEP 5: Pour all of the liquid into your hairspray bottle.

Use this as regular hairspray. You can experiment with spraying it on wet hair, like a volumizer, and blow-drying. Less is more.

The Future of Shampoo

Baby fine hair and thinning hair have specific shampoo needs -- at least as far as today's hair-care status quo is concerned. What did people do before the onslaught of personal care products? Will the future of hair care include so many potions?

At least one hair guru thinks the future of shampoo won't include shampoo at all!

"I honestly think in five years people are going to go, 'Oh God, remember when we used to wash our hair with shampoo?' " Michael Gordon, founder of

Bumble & Bumble hair-care line recently told *Wired* in "A Hair Salon Guru's Next Big Thing: Ending Shampoo." He isn't advocating for a return to a society with literally unwashed masses. Rather, he is describing his newest product line called Purely Perfect. The core idea of this product is simple: it is a balm with few ingredients you massage into your scalp and your hair strands, and then rinse out. That's it.

His inspiration is similar to the earlier section you just read on DIY hair-care products. He told *Wired* that he noticed that salon owners weren't using fancy shampoos on themselves and some of their clients. Instead, "They'd use a lot of grease, French hair-care stuff, face creams, they'd use sugar, they'd use soap, a lot of things -- but not normal hair products."

Beauty ... By Your Biome

A new, growing trend in hair and skin products relies on something that, well, might make you squeamish. Hang tight. This trend encourages the development, or rather redevelopment, of your skin's bacterial biome. Before you scream, "Eww!!!" take a second to check out "My No-Soap, No-Shampoo, Bacteria-Rich Hygiene Experiment," in *The New York Times*. After decades of trying to eliminate bacteria from our bodies we may have gone too far. We're just starting to learn about how bacterial species help keep our internal organs healthy.

Some people are going as far as eating probiotic rich foods (like yogurt and sauerkraut) to re-establish a healthy balance in their guts. As *The New York Times* reports, "companies like AOBiome are interested in how we can manipulate the hidden universe of organisms (bacteria, viruses and fungi) teeming throughout our glands, hair follicles and epidermis."

Similarly, several bacterial species actually work to keep our faces fresh and our tresses healthy. One reason our fine hair feels greasy so quickly is in part due to the health of our scalp. What if we could unlock the natural balance of bacteria and other species that keeps us cleaner longer? Some theorize that balding in men, and maybe women, is partially triggered by too much oil plugging up and then starving hair follicles on the scalp.

AOBiome is one new company that is developing products to encourage the establishment of friendly skin bacteria. Its founder is an interesting character who hasn't showered for several years

... and amazingly, has the reputation of not imparting a foul odor!

What can this potentially do for your hair? Time will tell. I'll be watching, will you? For latest developments on both of these trends, be sure to come to my website, FineHairSecrets.com.

Until Next Time

Thank you for reading this updated version of *Fine Hair Secrets*. I would appreciate you taking a few seconds and leaving me a review at Amazon.com. I'd like to hear to from you.

Connect with me at FineHairSecrets.com and join our mailing list for the latest tips, trends, and strategies for great hair and an even better life.

XOXO,
Holly

Made in the USA
Columbia, SC
05 May 2024

35306264R00046